ON YOUR OWN

Advice for Young Adults Leaving Home for the First Time

by
Jeffrey R. Caponigro

Barker
Books Inc.

On Your Own: Advice for Young Adults Leaving Home for the First Time

ISBN 0-9659606-3-3
Copyright © 2002 by Jeffrey R. Caponigro

Published by **Barker Books, Inc.**
4000 Town Center, Suite 900
Southfield, MI 48075

Jeffrey R. Caponigro

Leaving home for the first time is exciting. You finally escape the smothering blanket of your parents setting the rules, deciding on dinner, offering their opinions and seemingly watching your every move. But, leaving home for the first time is scary too. You soon find that you need to set your own rules, buy your own food, do your own laundry, make decisions based on your own judgment, and meet your responsibilities without the luxury of relying on someone else every step of the way. Homesickness often sets in as you realize that living with your parents wasn't that bad after all.

On Your Own was written to help young adults succeed as they venture on their own for the first time in their lives. It offers advice they probably ignored when their parents offered it, but now wish they had listened to. *On Your Own* is intended to be a helping hand, or guardian angel, for young adults as they leave home and walk into the unpredictable world of adulthood. And, it is intended to help parents feel better that their child has some guidance – in addition to themselves – as they let go of their most prized possessions.

I hope you enjoy the book.

Jeffrey R. Caponigro

Never guzzle,
swig or slam anything that
has alcohol in it.

Jeffrey R. Caponigro

Some mistakes
are easier to correct
than others.

Pass on the tattoo.

Jeffrey R. Caponigro

Learn to shake hands with people and
look them in the eyes with a smile.

You'll be surprised how quickly
they will take a liking to you.

6

Jeffrey R. Caponigro

Have a standard line to say
when someone offers you drugs.

"No thanks – I'll pass on it,"
seems to be as good as any.

People express their love for you
in different ways, but they rarely say
the words. Some say the words but don't
show it in their actions.

Remember that *actions* mean
more than *words*.

Jeffrey R. Caponigro

Make a practice of thinking ahead.
Keep yourself out of situations
that you may regret later.

Pick your battles.

Most things aren't worth
getting in a fight over.

Whⁿen travelling on an airplane,
ask for a window seat and enjoy how the clouds
look like marshmallows or a snowy field,
and appreciate the beauty of the water,
landscape and mountains.

Life is a series of compromises.

You'll never succeed at anything
if you insist on your own way
all the time.

Jeffrey R. Caponigro

Don't write anything
in an email note that would
embarrass you if published
on the front page
of your daily newspaper.

Work hard at really remembering
the names of those you meet.

People love to hear their names
repeated back to them.

No matter how smart, good looking
or rich you are, there's always someone
who is brighter, prettier or wealthier.

Don't get too hung up on yourself.

Never make fun of
the handicapped.

You could be in the
same position someday.

Read as much as you can.

It will improve your knowledge,
vocabulary, writing ability
and social skills.

Don't look at anything
on your computer screen that you
wouldn't if someone were looking
over your shoulder.

Trust your parents.
They just want to make sure
you don't make the same mistakes
they did when they were
your age.

Jeffrey R. Caponigro

Keep an open mind about people
who are different than you …
cultures you don't know much about …
and, opinions you're not
used to hearing.

The dumbest, most destructive
people in the world are those who feel
a specific race is superior to another.
Don't be dumb and destructive.

Jeffrey R. Caponigro

There are no shortcuts
to making money. People who have taken
shortcuts are in prison. Earn it honestly
and realize building wealth
takes time and patience.

Jeffrey R. Caponigro

Always thank the pilot and
flight attendant standing by the exit of the
airplane while you and others
are deplaning.

Understand your personal
comfort zone and challenge yourself
to push beyond it.

Y‌ou'll rarely get away with a lie
or something illegal. Fight the temptation,
even if you think no one will ever find out.

Someone almost always does.

Respect other people.
Never intimidate, harass, threaten
or abuse. You wouldn't want to be
treated that way.

Invest in your career.
Don't expect others to hand
anything to you.

Jeffrey R. Caponigro

Feel good about yourself
and people will feel the same way
about you.

The amount of money you'll make
in your first job after college
isn't nearly as important as what you'll learn,
the experience you'll gain
working with those you respect,
and the reputation of the company.
Be patient.

Don't generalize or stereotype.
It's no fun looking ignorant.

Jeffrey R. Caponigro

The way a person
handles himself is more
important than the size of his
bank account.

Don't trust gossip.
Give people the benefit of the doubt
until you know all the facts.

Jeffrey R. Caponigro

Everything that happens –
no matter how bad it seems at the time –
results in something positive down the road.
Keep the faith.

Don't be so quick to look for sex.
If you're going to have sex,
know your partner well and take
the proper precautions.

Are you prepared to accept a disease
or unwanted baby, if something
doesn't go the way you planned?

Learn to play golf to the best of your ability. It will help you in business down the road.

Try to find something to laugh hard
about every day. It's healthy for your psyche,
sense of humor and immune system.

Do some form of physical exercise
at least three times per week.

Jeffrey R. Caponigro

Eat in moderation.
Few people like being obese.

Jeffrey R. Caponigro

Use metaphors to
help explain something that's difficult
to get across. They can make things clear --
like wiping off a foggy mirror.

Jeffrey R. Caponigro

Few things hurt as much
as a toothache. And few things make you look
more attractive than good-looking teeth.
Visit a dentist for a checkup
every six months.

Jeffrey R. Caponigro

Be considerate of your roommates.
Keep the volume down
on the stereo.

Ensure a good grade in college
by studying hard, convincing yourself you like
the class and the subject, and making sure
the professor knows who you are.
Ask questions, participate in class and tell
the professor how much you
enjoy the class.

Volunteer to help out others
at a local senior-citizens center,
church or synagogue.
They need people like you.

Don't give away
punch lines to jokes, endings of movies
or the last chapters of books.

Call your friends to
just say "hi" every now and then.
Too many people let friends drift from
their lives and later regret it.

Be considerate of others.
Give up the remote control so others
can decide what to watch
once in a while.

Every business has customers.
Treat everyone you deal with like a customer
you want for life.

The very concept of recreational drugs is a fraud. Focus on non-destructive recreation such as swimming, golf, tennis, horseback riding, weight training or inline skating.

Adults who are janitors or
dry off cars at car washes wish they had
the same opportunities as you do now.
Don't underestimate the value
of your opportunities.

Whatever career you decide
to pursue, try to be the best you can be at it –
maybe even the best in the world.
And, realize that it takes hard work, discipline,
focus and commitment.

Long-term success isn't based
solely on achievements.
Avoid self-destruction. Don't let the stress
and temptations of life lead to
your failure.

Don't go to sleep without first
saying a prayer of thanks for what you have,
even if you think things could be better.

Jeffrey R. Caponigro

The older you get, the smarter you'll be.

Someday you'll look back
to your school days and regret that
you didn't try harder.

Don't gamble if
it will be too painful if you lose.
If you can't afford to lose, you can't afford
to risk trying to win.

If some older people seem cranky,
it's because they've run out of patience after
decades of seeing people like you
make dumb mistakes that could have been avoided.
It would make you cranky too.

Being a good role model
conveys more than anything
you could say in words.

Set aside some money
from each paycheck for
your savings account.

Keep in touch with your parents.
Help them make one of the biggest adjustments
of their lives. The fact you are no longer
living with them.

Everyone gets homesick, even those
who can't wait to leave home.
It's a sign that you're becoming an adult. You'll work
through it and be stronger for it.

Don't be afraid to visit a funeral home
when a friend, colleague or family member dies.
You being there means more
than you'll know.

If your company offers a 401(k) plan
with matching funds, invest as much as you can
afford and make sure you have
a balanced portfolio.

Much of who we are
is based on genetics and good fortune.
Be humble.

A thin line exists between
courage and stupidity. It may be gutsy to do
a handstand on a third-floor hotel balcony,
but it's also extremely stupid.
You would be amazed by how many people
die of stupidity each year.

Rejoice in the success of your friends
and relatives. Don't measure yourself against them.
Enjoy their success the way you would
want them to enjoy yours.

Remember the saying,
"you can't judge a book by its cover."
It's true. Get to know people
before making judgments.
You'd want them to do the same
when judging you.

If you are lucky enough
to still have your grandparents around,
stay in touch with them. They are proud of you
and like knowing that you still care.

Jeffrey R. Caponigro

Don't be in a hurry
to fall in love.
The best love grows
over time.

Jeffrey R. Caponigro

If you make a mistake that
creates a problem for someone, say you're sorry
and explain to the person what you
were thinking. Learn from the experience and
avoid making the same mistake again.

Jeffrey R. Caponigro

Treat waiters and waitresses
with respect. If you're not happy with the food
or service, politely tell them in person
after the meal or
write a note on the bill.

Jeffrey R. Caponigro

Skip the body piercing.
It likely won't send the message
you hope it will.

Jeffrey R. Caponigro

Write thank-you notes
to those who do something nice for you.
You'll be surprised
the positive impression that makes.

Read one new book
for enjoyment every
six months.

Jeffrey R. Caponigro

Don't allow the balance
on your credit card to ever exceed
one of your paychecks.
And, pay off the balance
as soon as possible.

Don't ever drive after
drinking alcohol or taking drugs.

Your life and the lives of others
can be ruined in a second – the time it takes
to make a wrong decision.

Don't carry all your cash
in your wallet or purse, in case it gets
stolen or misplaced.

Jeffrey R. Caponigro

Buy a photo album and save
pictures that you'll enjoy
seeing a few years down the road.

At least once every month,
try a new food that you previously thought
you would hate.
You'll be surprised what you'll end up liking.

Jeffrey R. Caponigro

Don't change a tire on a busy road.
Call for help.

Read a newspaper every day.
Don't rely solely on television or
radio to keep you informed.

Jeffrey R. Caponigro

Keep your shoes clean, your clothes neat,
and your hair and nails well groomed.
If you don't look like you have
your own act together, it is unlikely anyone
will take you too seriously.

When you are married
and have your first child, consider naming
the child after your father or mother.
It will mean a lot to them.

Jeffrey R. Caponigro

Don't expect others to be
responsible for your decisions. Pass on buying a pet
unless you really have the time and patience
to take care of it in good and bad times.

Jeffrey R. Caponigro

Always have a good
dictionary, calendar and calculator
near your computer.

Don't call someone
by a nickname that they
don't like.

Jeffrey R. Caponigro

Learn to wake up
in the morning without hitting
the snooze button.

Jeffrey R. Caponigro

Never ask for a raise or complain that you should be making more money. You're always better off determining what you could do to be more productive and make a stronger contribution. Then, work on those things and be patient. If you still aren't satisfied, then move on to another company. But leave with grace and gratitude – since you might want to return someday.

Look for opportunities
to compliment someone.
And, make a point of doing it.

Don't leave a shopping cart
in the middle of a parking lot.
You wouldn't like it if one rolled
into *your* car.

Jeffrey R. Caponigro

There are good and bad people
in all walks of life. Doctors, dentists, priests,
rabbis, preachers, college professors,
police officers, judges and business owners.
Don't blindly trust anyone, and stay away from
those who abuse their authority.

Be generous.
It always comes back to you
in some form of blessing.

If someone has just lost a friend
or relative, simply say, "I'm very sorry to hear that."
Responding to grief can be awkward
and uncomfortable, but won't be if you
remember that one line.

Jeffrey R. Caponigro

Learn to write well.
It will help in whatever
career you select.

Forget the goofy voice-mail
greeting at home. You never know when
your boss or a prospective employer
might be calling.
Stick with a standard, friendly greeting.

Earn the trust of those around you.
Start by always being on time, and calling
when you'll be more than
a few minutes late.

Maintain a consistent sleep cycle.
Try to go to bed about the same time each night
and wake up around the same time in the morning –
even on weekends.
You will get fewer colds, accomplish more during the
day and generally feel a lot better.

Jeffrey R. Caponigro

Write the lyrics to a song
or write a poem from scratch.
Then share them
with someone.

Jeffrey R. Caponigro

Don't ever think you're entitled to anything. Try to earn everything in life.

Jeffrey R. Caponigro

Think about how others might feel.
Don't throw your chewed gum
where someone might step on it, and definitely
don't stick it under the table
in a restaurant.

Make someone feel special.
Write a letter to your favorite teacher
from elementary school
and tell her how much you
appreciated the help.

Jeffrey R. Caponigro

Buy a new toothbrush
every two months, or anytime you catch a cold.
Throw the old one away or use it
to clean your shower.

Jeffrey R. Caponigro

Make your bed every morning.
A made bed always feels better when you
get into it at night.

Jeffrey R. Caponigro

Play it smart with your car.
Change the oil and rotate the tires
every 3,000 miles.

Jeffrey R. Caponigro

No one likes unpleasant surprises. Don't flush the toilet when your roommate is taking a shower.

Resist the temptation to use your car
as a weapon. No matter how enraged or in a
hurry you are, don't cut anyone off or follow
too closely. You don't know how the driver
of the other car will respond.

It only takes a second to show
someone your lack of maturity and intelligence.
Don't ever give anyone the finger,
no matter how upset you are.

Beginning with your first salaried position,
make it a practice to get to work
at least 30 minutes before you are expected to start
and stay 30 minutes longer than you are
expected to work. Doing so will help you stay
on top of your job, and will show others that you
will do what it takes to get the job done right.

Don't use your company's
letterhead to send your letter and resume
when looking for a new position
at another company.

Most things become easier
the more you do them. Find the occasion to
make a speech or talk in front of a large group
at least every four or five months.

Jeffrey R. Caponigro

Never have more than two
alcoholic drinks over the course of a
business dinner or reception,
no matter how many drinks
others may have.

When making a toast at a wedding
or rehearsal dinner, don't tell a story that will
embarrass the couple or their families.
Stick with something warm and classy,
and don't feel obligated to turn it into
a stand-up comedy routine.

Hold the elevator door open for women
and the elderly, and allow them to get on and off
the elevator first. A smile and a little nod
also is a nice touch.

Be considerate of others
at sporting events. Keep the crude comments
and vulgarities to yourself.

Jeffrey R. Caponigro

Many subjects that seemed like routine discussions with friends at school should be left out of the workplace. Don't curse with co-workers, show any disrespect for members of the opposite sex or discuss how you got totally wasted all weekend partying. Even if your boss does it, don't consider it an invitation to follow suit.

When leaving a voice-mail message
for someone, get to the point quickly but slow down
when saying your phone number.

Jeffrey R. Caponigro

Certain topics should not
be joked about. Stay away from wisecracks
about race, gender, suicide, religious beliefs,
the spouse or parents of a friend or colleague,
taking a weapon onto an airplane, or shootings
in school or at work.

Don't eat leftover egg salad
that no longer smells
like eggs.

Jeffrey R. Caponigro

If someone is upset with you and raising
his or her voice, don't let the emotion of the situation
get the best of you. Keep your cool and listen
intently to the core issues that you can address.
Apologize calmly to the person and then
explain how you arrived at the decision or the
action you took, suggest what you could do
to resolve it, and agree on how to handle
a similar situation the next time.

A place and a time exist for everything.
Don't talk in a theater after the movie
or play has started.

Everyone is different.
Don't criticize anyone for the music
they listen to, the food they eat,
the art they enjoy, and the people
whom they consider friends.

Jeffrey R. Caponigro

Don't be afraid of failure.
Consider what you would do in life if you knew
you couldn't fail at it. What would you attempt
if you knew for certain that you would
be hugely successful at it?
How great would you feel if you succeeded?
Don't assume failure. Assume success.
Go for it!

You always should be able to think
of three hobbies you have at any given time.
If you can't, you need to consider
some new interests to help make you a more
balanced and interesting person.

Carry yourself with good posture.
You will look more confident
and approachable.

Jeffrey R. Caponigro

If you feel yourself nodding off when driving,
immediately pull over in a safe location
away from a busy road or highway, lock your car doors
and rest until you feel okay to drive safely again.
Don't drive under any circumstances
if the reason you are tired is because you are under the
influence of alcohol or drugs.

Don't refer to anyone at work as Babe, Baby, Love, Sweetheart, Sweetie, Honey, Girlfriend, Cutie or any other name that doesn't belong in business.

Be gracious when given a compliment.
Many people have difficulty accepting
a compliment without disagreeing or explaining
why they could have done better.
Such a response often makes the person offering
the compliment feel uncomfortable.
"Thank you – I appreciate it" is always
the best response.

Jeffrey R. Caponigro

Keep impulse buying to a minimum.
Before you buy anything pricey that you
don't absolutely need, wait a day or two
to determine if you still think you must have it
and, in your opinion, if it is still
worth the money.

Never ask if someone is pregnant
unless you know with total certainty that she is.
Because you'll feel terrible if her response is,
"No. Why? Do I look fat or something?"

Jeffrey R. Caponigro

Be polite when pulled over
by a police officer.

Jeffrey R. Caponigro

Make sure to respond to an
invitation that reads "RSVP."

Don't ever park in a parking spot designated for the handicapped, unless you yourself have obtained a handicapped permit through the appropriate authorities.

When contacting a company for a job,
always treat secretaries and
executive assistants with the same respect
and manners that you would their bosses.
They will most assuredly offer opinions about you
to their bosses, who rely on their secretaries
or executive assistants for their
input and advice.

Always carry your drink
with you at a party. Never leave it unattended
where someone could put something in it
that you wouldn't want to drink.

You never know when you might
lose or leave behind something important.
Don't carry anything in your purse,
backpack, lunchbox or briefcase that would be
humiliating or get you into trouble
with the law if someone
else found it.

Be a dreamer. List five things you want to
accomplish in life and think through
how you can make them happen.

Jeffrey R. Caponigro

Remember how it felt when
people helped you --
parents when you were sick or needed money,
teachers in school, friends when you
needed support, references to get into college,
and help to get that first job.
Help out others when you have the
opportunity to do so.

Don't hold grudges.
If someone apologies to you, try to forget
what made you upset and give
him or her another chance.

Jeffrey R. Caponigro

Yου never know when you
will need the help of others. Be nice to everyone
with whom you come in contact.

Jeffrey R. Caponigro

Be prepared to accept
the consequences of your actions
and words. Don't write anything
anonymously that you
wouldn't want attributed to you.

Jeffrey R. Caponigro

Know all the information needed
to make a sound decision. Don't dive into a
swimming pool or lake without first testing
the depth of the water.

Don't ever consume more than one beer, glass of wine or alcoholic drink per hour.

Jeffrey R. Caponigro

Some things just don't go together.
Don't smoke while you're filling up
your car's gas tank.

Jeffrey R. Caponigro

Buy or make some note cards
to have handy for sending "thank you" cards
to those who do something nice for you.

Jeffrey R. Caponigro

Don't sleep overnight in a room
that you painted the same day.

Jeffrey R. Caponigro

The only answer to someone
who asks if he or she looks fat
in a specific outfit is, "No, not at all."
Anything further is guaranteed
to get you in trouble.

Learn to do at least one
card trick.

Jeffrey R. Caponigro

Before checking out of a hotel,
leave a tip in your room for the housekeeper
who probably works harder than anyone,
doesn't get paid much for doing it,
and certainly deserves a little extra
for cleaning up after you.

Don't chew gum in a job interview
or at the workplace.

When someone firmly says, "No,"
don't try to talk him or her into it.
This is especially important
when it involves sex, drugs or alcohol.

Jeffrey R. Caponigro

Work harder than the
average performer thinks
is necessary.

Don't be afraid of failing or
making a mistake. Positive results often occur
when you try but don't totally succeed.
The greater error is not trying
in the first place.

Jeffrey R. Caponigro

Don't use a nickname in your email address that would send the wrong message when communicating with someone important.

superstud@_____.com won't work any better when contacting a company for a job interview than *hard2please@____.com* will when asking someone out for a date.

If you're higher than six feet
from the ground, ask someone
to hold the ladder.

Consider your actions and how they
reflect on your parents and family.
Think again before doing something
you'll regret someday.

Be there when it counts most.
Stick up for someone who is being
abused or mistreated.

Jeffrey R. Caponigro

Turn off your cell phone
when you're in a church, synagogue,
funeral home, class, job interview
or with a customer.

Jeffrey R. Caponigro

Auto accidents are sometimes out of our control,
but it is possible to prevent death
or serious injury.

Always wear your seat belt and encourage
others with you to do the same.

No matter how you feel,
remember that more people
than you will ever realize are rooting for you.
Don't ever give up.

Jeffrey **R. Caponigro** is the father of two boys, Nick and Mike. He wrote *On Your Own* as his wife Ellen and he approached the years when their sons would move away from home themselves. He owns a public relations firm, Caponigro Public Relations Inc., with offices in Southfield and downtown Detroit, Michigan. He has counseled more than 350 different companies and organizations during his nearly 25 years in public relations.

Caponigro is the author of *The Crisis Counselor: The step-by-step guide to managing a business crisis* (©2000, McGraw Hill/Contemporary Books). He has helped manage more than 150 different crisis situations, and is considered one of the top crisis-management consultants in the United States. He earned his Accreditation from the Public Relations Society of America and was elected to the PRSA College of Fellows in 2001.

He earned a B.A. degree in English and journalism from Central Michigan University in Mount Pleasant, Mich., and serves on its Board of Trustees through 2008.

Learn more about Caponigro Public Relations Inc. on the Internet at www.caponigro.com or about his book *The Crisis Counselor* at www.crisiscounselor.com.

Jeff Caponigro's email address is jcap@caponigro.com. He would be pleased to hear from you.

On Your Own: *Advice for Young Adults Leaving Home for the First Time*

by Jeffrey R. Caponigro

Barker
Books Inc.

Southfield, Mich.